Breakfasts for Lovers

LU LOCKWOOD

Illustrated by Jill Coykendall Callaway

PEREGRINE PRESS
Old Saybrook, Connecticut

Manufactured in the United States of America

FIRST PRINTING

ISBN 0-933614-11-X

Table of Contents

Love Birds
French Seventy Fives, Quail in Orange Boats,
Squares of Pecan Bread *11*

Royal Wedding
English Beer, Filet Steaks, English Muffins, Poached Eggs,
Bernaise Sauce *13*

Downeast Dawn
White Wine, Finnan Haddie Soup, Toast Points, Lemon Wedges *15*

From Russia with Love
Hot Vodka Laced Tomato Juice with Sour Cream and Caviar,
Chicken Livers Veronique, Pumpernickle Melba *17*

Some Like It Hot
Margaritas, Mexican Eggs, Toasted Pita Bread *19*

Manhattan Affair
Pink Gin, Quiche Extraordinare *21*

April in Paris
Frothy Mocha Frappe, Layer Cake of Crepes, Jams, and Cream *23*

Brigadoon
Orange Carrot Shake, Flaming Scotch Oatmeal *25*

Prince of Hanover
Aristocratic Breakfast Punch, Goldenrod Eggs, Coronets of Ham,
German Rye Bread *27*

The Sheik
Sunflower Seed, Sunrise Shish Kabob on Toasted French Bread 29

Midnight Sun
Vodka Firefly, Seafood Patties with Dill Egg Sauce 31

Hawaiian Lovesong
Papaya Champagne, Cheese Stuffed with Many Things 33

Southern Gentleman
Mint Julep, Mushroom Roll, Smoked Ham with
Hollandaise Sauce, Bloody Mary Muffins 35

It's the Berries
Strawberry Delight, French Finger Sandwiches 37

Helen of Troy
Ouzo and Apricot Juice, Moussaka Omelette, Hard Rolls 39

Mexican Holiday
Strawberries and Rum, Mushrooms el Presidente 41

Southern Dream
Sillabub, Corn and Sausage Pie 43

Irish Morning
Irish Coffee, The Great Irish Potato with Bacon and Eggs 45

Sleepy Island
Rum Swizzle, Baked Sausage in Crescent French Toast
with Maple Syrup 47

Marriage of Figaro
Marriage of Figaro, Angels on Horseback, Tiny Omelettes 49

Catherine the Great
Clam and Boullion Topped with Vodka Cream,
Smoked Salmon Coubliac *51*

Eve's Downfall
Happy Apple Juice, Beef Benedict *53*

Days of Wine and Roses
Racey Wine, Love Roses on Toasted English Muffins *55*

Fiery Passion
Red Sea, Toast, Pimiento, Cheese and Caviar *57*

Big Sur
Bellini, California Omelette, Parsley Buttered Toast *59*

Rendezvous
Lite Beer, Morning Paté with Corn Bread *61*

Sunrise in Vermont
Sunshine Wine, Emperor's Pancakes *63*

Lovely Liaison
Chablis, Cheese Soufflé, Melba Toast, Snappy Apples *65*

Canadian Courtship
Poached Pears in Wine, Breakfast Kedgeree, French Bread Slices *67*

Georgia on My Mind
Bourbon Punch, Potato Cakes, Eggs, Peanut Sauce *69*

Pas de Deux
Wild Strawberry Wine, Poached Eggs in Maple Syrup,
Real French Toast *71*

Introduction

The critical period in matrimony is breakfast-time.
> A.P. Herbert: *Uncommon Law*

Serenely full, the epicure would say
"Fate cannot harm me, I have dined today."
> Sydney Smith: *A Recipe For Salad*

I have been cooking professionally for more than forty years, and all during that time I have always had a special affinity for that most standard (and frequently mundane) of meals: breakfast.

People will look forward to a fine gourmet dinner for weeks, but how many even consider an elegant, easily prepared gourmet breakfast, made in their own kitchen and savored there, or on the patio, or even in the bedroom. Couples should approach breakfast not as a thing to get through so that they can face the rigors of the day, but rather as an *experience,* an opportunity to enjoy each other's company, to renew their relationship, and to share a succulent meal together. If Romeo and Juliet had enjoyed long, leisurely gourmet breakfasts, things might not have ended so tragically.

The recipes included in this book have all been extensively tested, and many of them have been on the menu at one or another of my restaurants, usually as a brunch selection. In many cases, some or all of the ingredients can be prepared ahead of time — these will be obvious.

So, lovers, relax and enjoy that rarity of rarities, a GREAT breakfast. I'm sure you'll find your life and your love enriched.

LU LOCKWOOD

Love Birds

French Seventy Fives
Quail in Orange Boats
Squares of Pecan Bread

Champagne
Brandy
Sugar Cubes
Quail
Oranges
Honey
Currant Jelly
Orange Juice
Salt
Flour
Baking Powder
Butter
Apple Brandy
Pecans
Eggs
Cream

French Seventy Fives

In 2 flute glasses place 1 sugar cube in bottom of each and pour in each 1 ounce brandy. Let soak until sugar dissolves. Fill each with chilled champagne when ready to serve.

Quail in Orange Boats

Cut 2 large thin skinned oranges in half and scoop out insides (dispose of seeds). Keep orange shells. Place insides in a blender with 2 tablespoons honey and 2 tablespoons currant jelly. Blend well.

Salt 2 quails inside and out, and set in an orange half. Divide sauce, and pour over all. Place other half orange shell on top, set the 2 oranges in a souffle dish in 1 cup orange juice. Bake in 350° oven 1-1/2 to 2 hours. Remove orange lid to test quail. Be certain that orange shell is also tender as it may also be eaten.

Pecan Bread

In a bowl, mix 1-1/2 cups flour, 2 teaspoons baking powder, 2 tablespoons melted butter, 2 beaten eggs, 1/2 cup cream, 1/4 cup apple brandy, and 1 cup pecans. Grease muffin tins and bake at 350° for 35 minutes. Makes 6.

11

Royal Wedding

English Beer
Grilled Filet Steak on English Muffins
topped with Poached Eggs and Bernaise Sauce

Filet Steak
English Muffins
Eggs
Butter
Shallots
Tarragon Vinegar
Tarragon
Salt
White Pepper
Parsley
English Beer

Poached Eggs

Fill a deep saucepan 3/4 full of water, add 2 tablespoons white vinegar, and 1 teaspoon salt. Bring to a boil and lower heat just enough to keep water at a high simmer. Place 4 eggs in 4 cups. Take a table knife and swirl water; keep water swirling around by rolling knife around edge of water. Gently slip each cup in water and let egg slide out. When all four are in water, keep swirling for 4 minutes. Turn off heat, remove egg with a slotted spoon and set in cold water. Take scissors and, holding each egg, carefully trim off edges.

English Muffins

Butter English muffins, and set under broiler.

Grilled Filet Steak

Cut 1 pound filet mignon steak into 4 pieces. Melt 2 tablespoons of butter in skillet, and grill steaks quickly, turning once. Place on muffins, top each steak with egg. Place in 200° oven and hold.

Bearnaise Sauce

Melt 1/4 cup butter in skillet. Hold. Place 2 chopped and peeled shallots, 1 tablespoon tarragon vinegar, and 1/2 teaspoon dried tarragon in a small saucepan, and cook until liquid dissolves. Whisk 2 egg yolks and 1-1/2 tablespoons water. Add eggs to tarragon mixture, mix well, place over heat. Whisking all the time, add butter, 1 spoon at a time. Pour over eggs and steak.

Fill 2 tall pilsner glasses with a good English Beer.

13

DOWNEAST DAWN

Chilled White Wine
Finnan Haddie Soup
Toast Points & Lemon Wedges

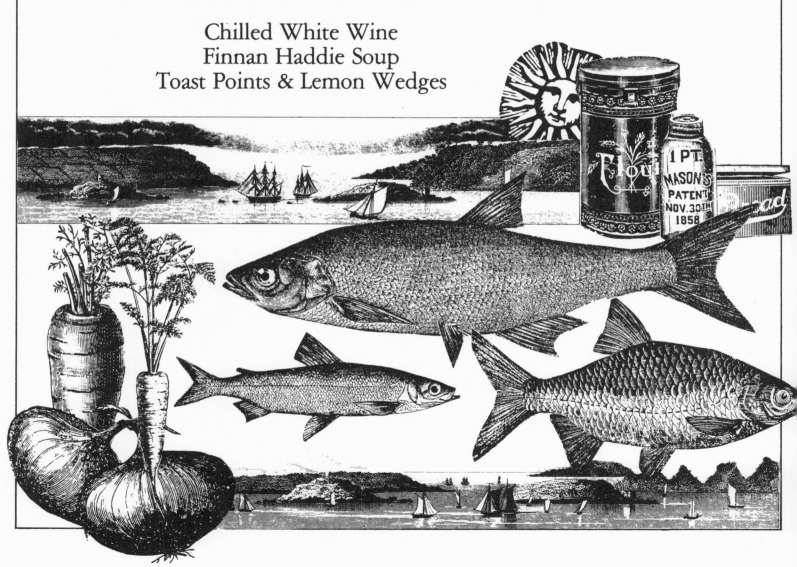

Lemon
Finnan Haddie
Milk
Oil
Leek
Carrot
Onion
Unsalted Butter
Flour
Cheesecloth Bag
Garlic Clove
Parsley
Peppercorns
Dried Thyme
White Fish Stock
Cream
Salt
White Pepper
Vermouth
White Bread
Chilled White Wine

Finnan Haddie Soup

In a saucepan, combine 1 pound finnan haddie (smoked haddock), 2 cups water, and 1 cup heavy cream. Simmer 20 minutes. Transfer fish, dividing evenly between 2 large rim soup bowls. Save creamy water. In a skillet, add 1 tablespoon oil over low heat. Chop fine: 1 peeled carrot, 1 leek, and 1 small onion. Add to oil, stirring constantly until soft. Add creamy water, 1 teaspoon dill, 1 teaspoon salt, 1 teaspoon white pepper, and a cheesecloth bag of garlic, parsley, peppercorns, and dried thyme. Simmer 30 minutes. Cool. Add 1/2 cup heavy cream, and 1/4 cup vermouth. Puree in blender, return to stove, heat well and pour over fish.

Toast Points and Lemon Wedges

Toast 3 slices of white bread, cut into triangles, and set in linen napkin in basket, covering toast to keep warm. Dunk in the soup.

Cut 2 lemons into 6 wedges each. Put out for both soup and wine.

Pour chilled white wine into tall stemmed white wine glasses.

15

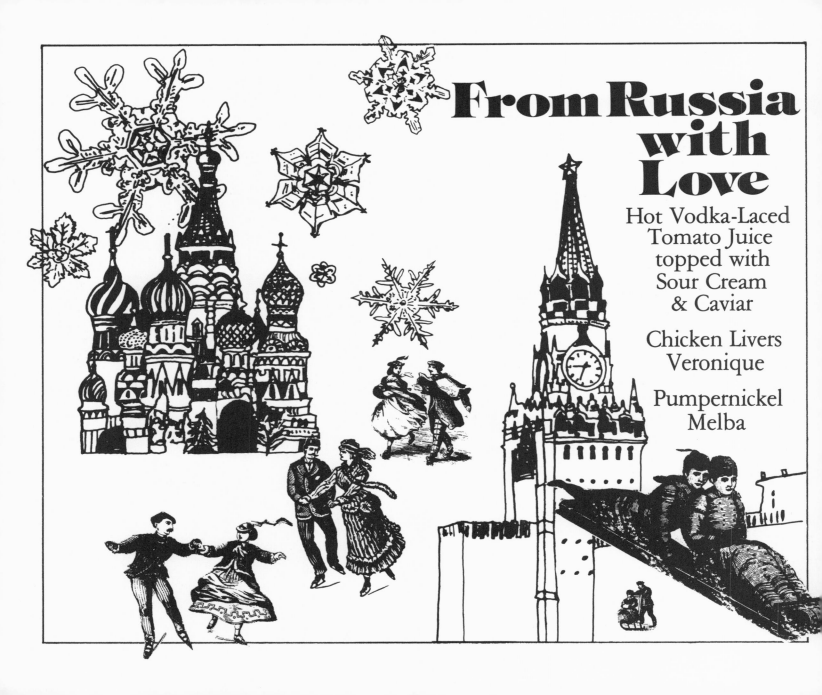

From Russia with Love

Hot Vodka-Laced
Tomato Juice
topped with
Sour Cream
& Caviar

Chicken Livers
Veronique

Pumpernickel
Melba

Chicken Livers
Butter
Salt
Pepper
Flour
Cream
Dry Vermouth
Seedless White Grapes
Pumpernickel Bread
Tomato Juice
Worcestershire Sauce
Tabasco
Vodka
Sour Cream
Caviar

Pumpernickel Melba

Use pumpernickel bread sliced paper thin. Cover cookie sheet with slices, cutting each one in half diagonally. Spread melted butter on each piece with a pastry brush. Bake at 350° for 15 minutes; remove and cool.

Chicken Livers Veronique

In a skillet, melt 3 tablespoons butter. Dust chicken livers in salt, pepper, and flour. Sauté until thoroughly cooked, remove, and set aside. Add 1 teaspoon flour (with salt and pepper) to skillet and wisk around until flour disappears. Slowly add 1/4 cup cream and 1/4 cup dry vermouth, and whisk until you have a creamy sauce. Add livers and 1 cup grapes, and simmer for a few minutes.

Divide chicken liver mixture, and serve in soup bowls. Place pumpernickel melba around the edge of the bowls.

Hot Vodka-Laced Tomato Juice

To 4 cups of tomato juice, add 2 teaspoons Worcestershire, 1 teaspoon tabasco, and 4 ounces vodka. Heat slowly and serve in giant coffee cups topped with 1 tablespoon sour cream and 1 teaspoon caviar.

17

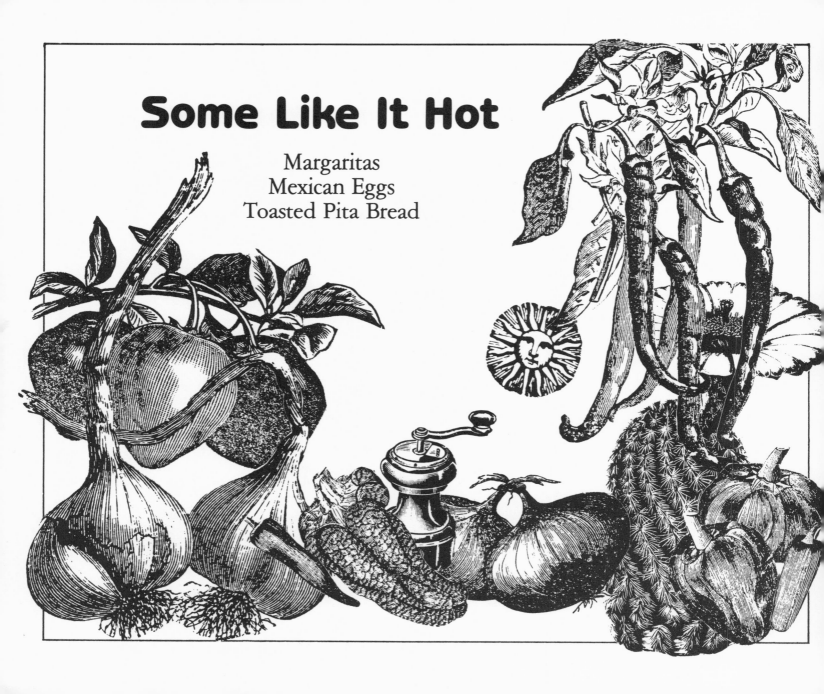

Some Like It Hot

Margaritas
Mexican Eggs
Toasted Pita Bread

Pita Bread
Butter
Seasoned Salt
Green Pepper
Pimiento
Eggs
Heavy Cream
Salt
Pepper
Oil
Garlic
Cayenne Pepper
Red Hot Sauce
Parmesan Cheese
Parsley
Triple Sec
Tequila
Lime Juice
Salt

Mexican Eggs

In a skillet, add to 1/2 cup oil 1 crushed clove garlic, 1 diced green pepper, and 1 thinly sliced pimiento — saute gently. Put in a 1 quart casserole when slushy. Beat 4 eggs and add 1/2 cup heavy cream, 1 teaspoon salt, 1/2 teaspoon pepper, 1/4 teaspoon cayenne pepper, and 1/4 teaspoon red hot sauce. Pour in casserole. Set casserole into pan of water halfway up sides. Sprinkle 1/4 cup parmesan cheese and 1/4 cup chopped parsley mixed together. Bake in 375° oven for 40 minutes.

Toasted Pita Bread

Slit 2 pita breads in half, butter and sprinkle with seasoned salt. Set in 350° oven for 20 minutes until crispy.

Margaritas

Shake 2 ounces Triple Sec, 4 ounces tequila, 4 ounces lime juice with 2 cups shaved ice. Dip rims of 2 cocktail glasses in lime juice then into a flat dish of salt. Set in freezer to ice up, then strain mixture up to the salt edge.

19

MANHATTAN AFFAIR

Pink Gin
Quiche Extraordinaire

Bloody Mary Mix
Horseradish
Gin
Bread
Butter
Parmesan Cheese
Prepared Pie Crust
Tiny Shrimp
Zucchini
Swiss Cheese
Parsley
Eggs
Cream
Dill
Salt and Pepper

Pink Gin

Mix 1 bottle Bloody Mary mix, 1 teaspoon horseradish and 1 cup gin. Chill. Serve in large glasses on which the following will float. Cut 2 large circles from white bread. Melt 1 tablespoon butter in skillet with 1 teaspoon Parmesan cheese, and sauté bread on both sides. Let dry about 10 minutes.

Quiche Extraordinaire

In a prepared pie crust, place a layer of grated Swiss cheese. Then add a layer of cooked tiny shrimp, a layer of cooked zucchini slices, and another thin layer of grated Swiss cheese. Beat 4 eggs with 1 cup cream and a dash of cayenne pepper, parsley and dill. Gently pour over pie. Bake at 400° for 30 minutes or until knife comes out smoothly.

21

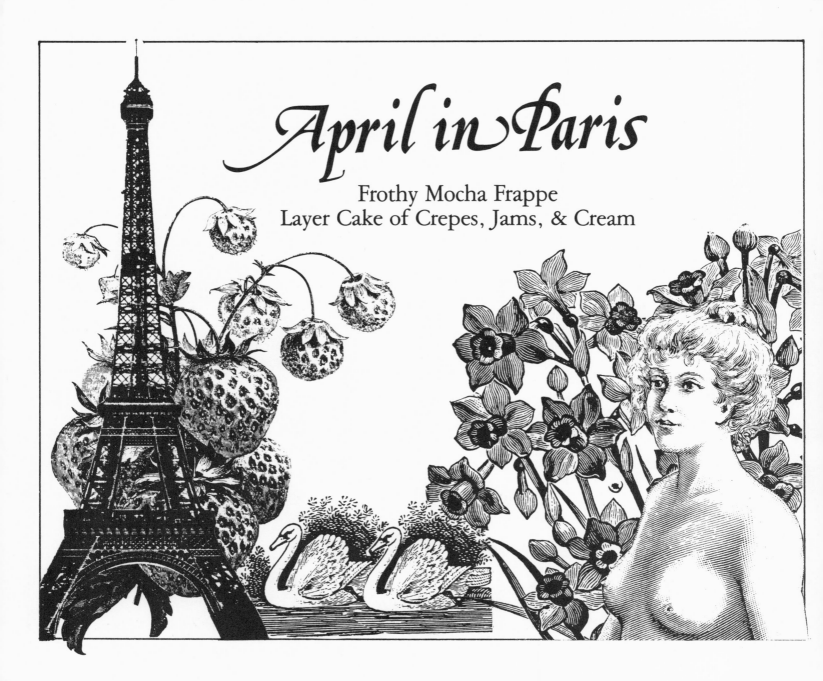

April in Paris

Frothy Mocha Frappe
Layer Cake of Crepes, Jams, & Cream

Coffee
Instant Cocoa
Eggs
Creme de Cacao
Chocolate Liqueur
Crepes*
Currant Jam
Strawberries
Apples
Guava Jelly
Fine Sugar
Butter
Cream
Strawberry Liqueur
Calvados

Frothy Mocha Frappe

Heat 2 cups of hot strong coffee, and pour in 1 package of instant cocoa. Cool. In a blender, add 1/2 cup cream, 2 teaspoons fine sugar and coffee cocoa mixture. Blend well for 2 minutes. Add 1 tablespoon creme de cacao and 1 tablespoon chocolate liqueur, blend 2 more minutes. Refrigerate until ready to serve. Serve in mugs, and top with whipped cream.

Layer Cake of Crepes, Jams & Cream

Peel 2 apples and dice. Melt 2 tablespoons butter and 1 teaspoon fine sugar. Add apples and saute until tender. Cool and set aside. Wash and slice a small box of strawberries. Sprinkle with fine sugar and set aside.

Lay out 10 crepes. Cover 1 with guava jelly, put a crepe on top, and cover with half the apple mixture, then cover with another crepe, and spread with more guava jelly. Continue to layer as follows: put another crepe on top and spread with half the strawberry mixture, cover with a crepe, spread with currant jelly and cover with another crepe, then apple, crepe, currant jelly, crepe, strawberry, crepe, guava jelly, crepe. Press down gently. Place in 350° oven for 10 minutes. Beat 1 pint cream with 1 tablespoon strawberry liqueur, 1 teaspoon fine sugar, 1 teaspoon calvados. Serve crepe warm, cut in wedges with a bowl of the whipped cream.

*See Sunrise in Vermont

23

BRIGADOON

Orange Carrot Shake

Flaming Scotch Oatmeal with
Honey, Banana
& Frozen Yogurt

Orange
Carrot Juice
Dry Vermouth
Honey
Scotch Oatmeal
Scotch Whiskey
Wheat Germ
Banana
Frozen Yogurt

Orange Carrot Shake

Blend the juice of 1 orange, 1 small can of carrot juice, 2 tablespoons dry vermouth, and 1 teaspoon honey. Chill and serve in red wine glasses.

Flaming Scotch Oatmeal

Follow directions on a good brand of oatmeal. After it's cooked, scoop into rim soup bowls. Sprinkle wheat germ, 1/2 sliced banana, and drizzle honey over all. Warm 1/2 cup Scotch whiskey, and divide over the 2 bowls. Ignite, top with frozen yogurt and die of Joy!

25

Prince of Hanover

Aristocratic Breakfast Punch
Goldenrod Eggs
Coronets of Ham
& German Rye Bread

Burgundy
Brandy
Champagne
Sparkling Water
Ice Cubes or Mold
Cube Sugar
Lime
Flour
Butter
Eggs
Worcestershire Sauce
Cream
Salt
German Rye Bread
Baked Ham
Parsley

Aristocratic Breakfast Punch

In a glass pitcher pour 1 small bottle burgundy, 1/4 cup brandy, 1/2 bottle champagne and 7 ounces sparkling water. Set in freezer for 30 minutes. Fill a small punch bowl with ice cubes and 1 lime thinly sliced. Pour drink over ice. Serve in punch cups with a sugar cube in each.

Goldenrod Eggs

Hard-boil 4 eggs. Peel, cool and chop. Melt 3 tablespoons butter, add 2 tablespoons flour, and mix well. Add 1 cup cream and 1/2 teaspoon Worcestershire sauce. Blend in chopped eggs and salt to taste.

Coronets of Ham & German Rye Bread

With rolling pin, roll out 4 slices trimmed German rye bread. Place 2 thin slices of baked ham on each bread slice. Roll up like a cigar, brush with melted butter, and bake at 350° for 30 minutes or until golden brown, turning once.

Set 2 ham coronets on plates, and divide egg sauce over all. Garnish with chopped parsley.

27

the sheík

Sunflower Seed
Sunrise Shish Kabob on
Toasted French Bread

Italian Sweet Sausage
Cherry Tomatoes
Whole Mushrooms
Green Pepper
French Bread
Butter
Garlic
Shish Kabob Skewers
Vodka
Grapefruit Juice
Honey

Sunrise Shish Kabob

Cut 6 Italian fennel and sage sweet sausages into 12 pieces. Wash and dry 4 large mushrooms and 4 cherry tomatoes. Cut 1 green pepper into 4 squares. Put sausage and vegetables alternately on skewers. Place on baking sheet and cook in 425° oven for 15 minutes.

Cut 2 pieces (6'' long) from a loaf of French bread. Cut down the middle, and open up. Melt 4 tablespoons butter in a skillet with 1 minced garlic clove. Brush bread well with butter and set in oven for last 5 minutes of Shish Kabob.

Lay Shish Kabobs down middle of one side of bread, pull out skewer, and top with the other piece of bread. Press down gently.

Sunflower Seed

In a blender, place 16 ounces grapefruit juice, 2 ounces honey, and 6 ounces vodka. Blend 2 minutes or until all snappy taste is out of the grapefruit juice. Refrigerate until served. Serve in tall glasses with ice.

Midnight Sun

Vodka Firefly
Seafood Patties with Dill Egg Sauce

Vegetable Juice
Vodka
Worcestershire Sauce
Sauce Robert
Sole
Scallops
Shrimp
Egg Whites
Cream (light)
Parsley
Shallots
Mushrooms
Tabasco
Butter
Flour
Clam Broth (bottled)
Eggs
Dill
Mace
Watercress

Vodka Firefly

Mix together 16 ounces of vegetable juice, 6 ounces vodka, 1/2 teaspoon Worcestershire sauce, 1 teaspoon Sauce Robert. Chill, shake and serve in pilsner glasses.

Seafood Patties

In a food processor, blend 1/2 pound sole, 1/2 pound scallops, 1/2 pound tiny shrimp, 1/4 cup mushrooms, 2 shallots, 1/4 tablespoon parsley, 2 egg whites, and 1/2 cup cream. *Chill 2 hours.* Make small patties and saute in butter.

Dill Egg Sauce

Melt 2 tablespoons butter and add 2 tablespoons flour, 1/2 cup light cream, 1/2 cup clam broth, 1 teaspoon dill, 1/2 teaspoon salt, 1/2 teaspoon pepper, dash of Tabasco, and 4 finely chopped hard boiled eggs. Mix, add a dash of mace, and serve over patties. Decorate with watercress.

31

HAWAIIAN LOVE SONG

Papaya Champagne
Cheese Stuffed with Many Things

Champagne
Papaya
Oil
Cheddar Cheese
Ground Pork
Ripe Olives
Onion
Tomatoes
Garlic
Coriander
Walnuts
Salt
Pepper
Egg
White Bread
Parsley

Papaya Champagne

In a blender, pour 1 bottle domestic champagne, 1 cup crushed ice, and 1 peeled, deseeded papaya. Blend well, pour into a glass pitcher, set in freezer for 20 minutes. Serve in iced champagne glasses.

Cheese Stuffed with Many Things

Oil 4 custard cups. Line bottom and sides with cheddar cheese slices leaving some excess to fold over top.

In a skillet heat 1 tablespoon of oil; add 1 cup minced onion and cook slightly. Add 1 minced garlic clove, 1 pound ground pork, 1/2 cup ripe olives, 1/2 teaspoon coriander, 1/2 cup chopped walnuts, 1 teaspoon salt and 1/2 teaspoon pepper. Cook gently 20 minutes.

Hard boil 1 egg. Peel, cool and cut into 4 lengthwise wedges. Scoop meat mixture into cheese cups half way, place 1/4 egg on meat, cover with more meat mixture, and fold cheese over top until well covered. Bake at 350° for 30 minutes.

Toast and trim off crusts of 4 slices of white bread. Set 2 slices on each plate, place slices of tomato on toast and top with stuffed cheese.

33

Southern Gentleman

Mint Julep
Mushroom Roll
Smoked Ham with Hollandaise
Bloody Mary Muffins

Bloody Mary Muffins

In a bowl place 1-3/4 cups sifted all-purpose flour. Add 1 egg, 3 tablespoons melted butter, 3/4 teaspoon salt, 2 teaspoons baking powder, 1 tablespoon sugar, 3/4 cup good Bloody Mary mix with 1 ounce of vodka, and stir gently. Pour batter into well greased muffin pan and bake at 400° for 30 minutes. Makes 6.

Hollandaise Sauce

Melt 2 cups of butter. Whisk 3 egg yolks and 3 tablespoons of cold water together. Place in a sauce pan over high heat and whisk quickly. Remove from heat, add butter, and whisk for 5 more minutes, adding 2 tablespoons lemon juice, 1/4 teasoon salt, and 1/2 teaspoon white pepper. Set aside.

Mushroom Roll

Finely chop 3/4 pound fresh mushrooms and dry well by wringing in tea towel. Add 1 tablespoon lemon juice and 4 tablespoons melted butter to the mushrooms. Separate 3 eggs. Beat yolks well, then beat whites very stiff. Place mushroom mixture in a bowl, whisk in the yolks and fold in egg whites. On a cookie sheet place a piece of well oiled foil shaped into a 6'' x 10'' oblong. Spread mushroom mixture into foil. Place in 350° oven for 15 minutes. Take out and let cool for 5 minutes. Lift 10'' side of foil and start to roll like a jelly roll. (If it sticks, loosen with a knife and shake foil.)

On a serving tray place 4 slices of smoked ham and set in a 200° oven to warm. Cut mushroom roll into 4 slices, place over ham, and pour hollandaise sauce over all.

Mint Julep

In each of 2 tall glasses muddle well 3 mint leaves, 1 teaspoon sugar and 2 teaspoons water. Fill the glasses with ice cubes. Pour bourbon over ice, stir, and garnish with sprigs of mint.

35

It's The Berries!

Strawberry Delight
French Finger Sandwiches

Strawberries (fresh)
Strawberries (frozen)
Strawberry Liqueur
Sour Cream
White Bread
Bacon
Eggs
Butter
Salt
Mace
Bean Sprouts
Port Wine

French Finger Sandwiches

Cook 8 slices of bacon until crisp, but left in shape. Hard-boil 4 eggs, place in a bowl, mash well and mix in 1 tablespoon butter, 1/2 teaspoon salt and 1/2 teaspoon mace, and last, add 1/4 cup sour cream. Spread on 4 slices of bread, put on bacon, another slice of bread and press down. Cut into finger shaped sandwiches and sprinkle with bean sprouts.

Strawberry Delight

Wash and divide 1 pint box fresh strawberries into 2 large wine glasses. Put 1/2 box frozen strawberries in blender and combine with 1/2 cup port wine and 1/2 cup strawberry liqueur. Blend and pour in glasses over fresh strawberries and top with sour cream. Serve with a spoon.

37

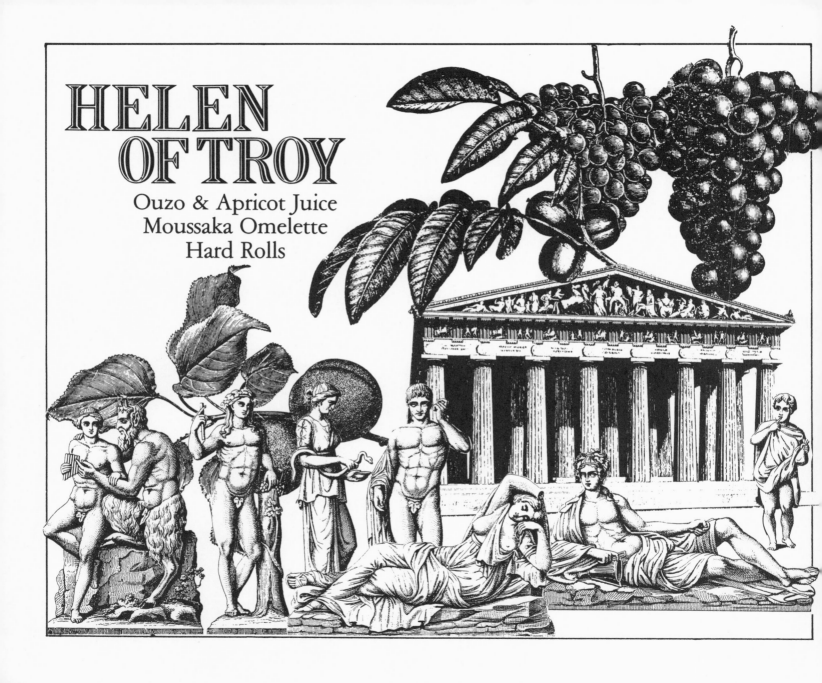

HELEN OF TROY

Ouzo & Apricot Juice
Moussaka Omelette
Hard Rolls

Ouzo
Apricot Juice
Almond Extract
Eggs
Milk
Butter
Cooked Lamb
Tomato
Green Pepper
Feta Cheese
Dill
Hard Rolls
Potato

Moussaka Omelette

Separate 6 eggs. To the yolks, add 1 teaspoon salt and beat. Beat egg whites until stiff and fold into egg yolks. Using an omelette pan, place 1 teaspoon butter and 1/2 of the egg mixture, cook 2 minutes and add filling. Flip 1/2 omelette over the filling. Serve hot.

Filling: In a food processor, blend together 1 peeled and chopped baking potato, 1 cup cooked lamb, 1 chopped green pepper, 1 peeled tomato, 1 garlic clove, 1/4 pound feta cheese and 1 egg. Place in a skillet and fry until it turns golden brown. Add a pinch of dill.

Heat French hard rolls and serve with lots of butter.

Ouzo & Apricot Juice

Combine 4 ounces of Ouzo, 10 ounces of apricot juice, 1 tablespoon honey and 1/4 teaspoon almond extract. Shake well with lots of ice and serve in a wine glass.

39

MEXICAN HOLIDAY

Strawberries & Rum
Mushrooms el Presidente

Mushrooms
Pita Bread
Pepper Cheese
Tomato
Butter
Rum
Strawberries
Sour Cream
Brown Sugar

Strawberries & Rum

Wash and stem 1 small box of strawberries. Place in a bowl and cover with 1 cup light rum. Sprinkle 2 tablespoons brown sugar on top and refrigerate.

Mushrooms el Presidente

Cut a tiny top off 2 pieces of pita bread. Lay out on foil large enough to wrap each one well. In a skillet, melt 2 tablespoons of butter and add 1 pound sliced mushrooms; sauté. Cube 2 tomatoes and 1/2 pound pepper cheese and combine with mushrooms. Divide in half and stuff pitas full. Push tops on, wrap in foil and bake at 400° for 30 minutes.

Remove strawberries from refrigerator. Put into bowls, top with sour cream and enjoy!

41

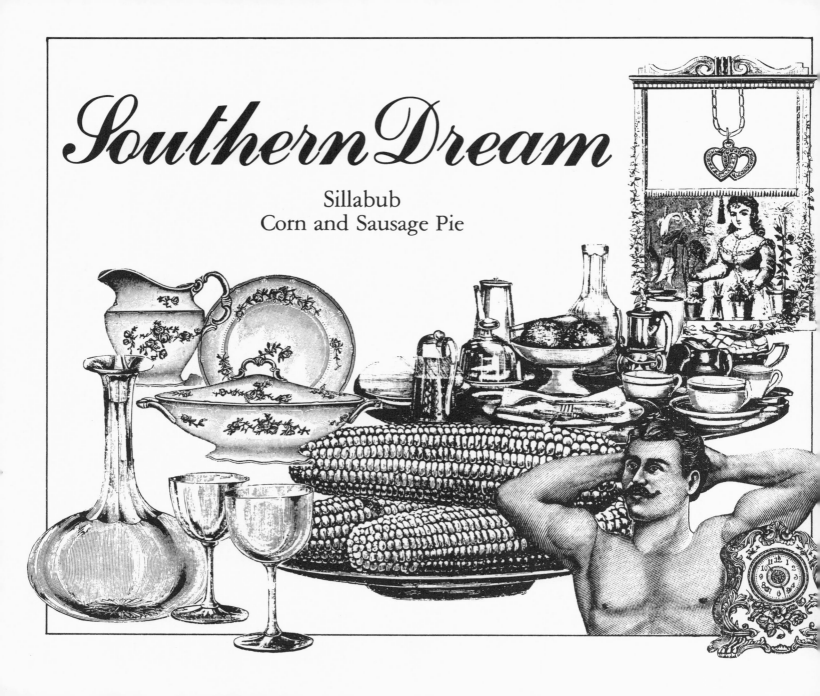

Southern Dream

Sillabub
Corn and Sausage Pie

Sherry
Brandy
Cream
Lemon
Fine Sugar
Corn Muffin Mix
Brown and
Serve Sausage
Butter

Sillabub

Grate the rind of a lemon as thinly as possible into 1/2 pint sherry (or Madeira), and *let stand for 12 hours*. Strain and add 3/4 pint cream, 2 tablespoons brandy, juice of one lemon and powdered or fine sugar to taste. Whisk: as froth forms, skim it off, and place in glasses. Refrigerate for a few hours before serving.

Corn and Sausage Pie

Grease a round bake pan with butter. Mix 2 packages of corn muffin mix. Spread half the batter in the pan, and lay sausages in the pan from outside edge pointing toward the center. Cover with the remaining batter, and bake according to directions. Slice like a pie and serve with lots of butter.

43

írísh morníng

Irish Coffee
The GREAT Irish Potato
with Bacon and Eggs

Large Baking Potatoes
Eggs
Bacon
Butter
Oil
Salt
White Pepper
Chopped Chives
Sour Cream
Dry Vermouth
Irish Whiskey
Strong Coffee
Heavy Cream
Fine Sugar
Mint Sprigs

The GREAT Irish Potato

Scrub 2 potatoes and rub with oil. Bake 1 hour in 400° oven. Fry 6 slices of bacon until crisp; dry and crumble. Save bacon fat. Beat 3 eggs, add 2 teaspoons chopped chives, 1 teaspoon salt, 1 teaspoon white pepper, 2 tablespoons cream, and 2 tablespoons dry vermouth. Pour into skillet of bacon fat, and soft scramble.

Lay potato on side and slice off top. Scoop out insides adding 1 tablespoon of butter and mash well. Add potato and bacon to egg mixture in skillet and mix well. Put the mixture into potato jacket (some will overflow) and replace top. Reheat in oven for 10 minutes.

Irish Coffee

In 2 Irish whiskey glasses, put 1 ounce of Irish whiskey in each and fill almost to the top with hot, strong coffee. Beat 1 cup of heavy cream with 2 teaspoons of fine sugar. Place heaps of the whipped cream on the coffee mixture and garnish each with a sprig of mint. Serve hot.

45

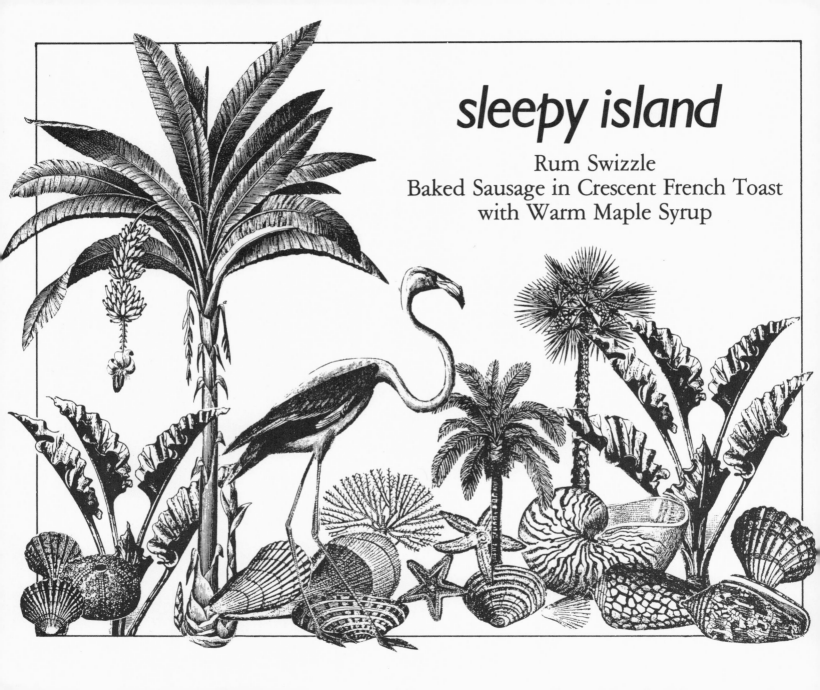

sleepy island

Rum Swizzle
Baked Sausage in Crescent French Toast
with Warm Maple Syrup

Can of Crescent Rolls
Link Sausage
Eggs
Butter
Maple Syrup
100 Proof Rum
Ginger Ale
Limes
Swizzle Stick

Baked Sausage in Crescent French Toast
Open can of crescent rolls and lay each one out flat on a baking sheet. Bake at 400° for 7 minutes. At the same time, place 8 sausages on a separate baking sheet, and bake 15 to 20 minutes.

Place a sausage on wide end of crescent and roll gently and a little loose. Wisk 3 eggs in sauce dish, adding 2 tablespoons cream, and dip each crescent in egg mixture. Melt 4 tablespoons butter in a big skillet, put crescents in and brown on all sides. Serve with warm maple syrup.

Rum Swizzle
In 2 tall glasses, add 1 ounce of rum to each. Fill with ice and add several lime slices. Pour in ginger ale and swizzle. Swizzle every once in a while to keep fizzy.

47

Marriage of Figaro

The Marriage of Figaro
Angels on Horseback
Tiny Omelettes

Oysters
Butter
Salt
Dry Vermouth
White Bread
Eggs
Chives
Parsley
Sparkling Burgundy
Champagne

Angels on Horseback
In a skillet place 2 tablespoons butter, 1/2 teaspoons salt, and 2 tablespoons dry vermouth. Melt and stir over low heat. Add 12 small shucked oysters, cover, and poach for 10 minutes. Remove oysters and set aside.

Take 4 pieces of trimmed white bread and fry until brown in the oyster pan to give the bread a good flavor. Set toast on a baking sheet and set 3 oysters on one side of each slice. Put in 200° oven to keep hot.

Tiny Omelettes
Separate 6 eggs. To the yolks, add 1/4 cup chopped chives and 1 teaspoon salt and beat. Beat egg whites until stiff and fold into egg yolks. Using a small crepe pan, place in it 1 teaspoon butter and 1/4 egg mixture, cook 2 minutes, and flip over. Remove, place in oven on toast, and repeat 3 more times. Sprinkle generously with chopped parsley.

Marriage of Figaro
One person holds the sparkling burgundy and the other holds the champagne. Each crosses arms filling tall chilled champagne glasses 1/2 full. Switch bottles and fill the opposite glass so you have a marriage of the wines.

49

CATHERINE The GREAT

Clam and Boullion
Topped with Vodka Cream

Smoked Salmon Coubliac

Clam Juice
Boullion
Vodka
Cream
Smoked Salmon
Onions
Sour Cream
Caviar
Eggs
Puff Pastry

Clam and Boullion Topped with Vodka Cream

In a saucepan, heat 1 can boullion with 1 bottle clam juice. Keep on simmer. Beat 1/2 pint heavy cream and fold in 1/2 cup vodka. Combine with the clam juice mixture and set in the refrigerator. Serve in large wine glasses.

Smoked Salmon Coubliac

Make your own puff pastry, or buy a good one. Roll out 4 pieces to form a 5'' x 7'' oblong (quite thin). In the center of the pastry (leaving enough edges to fold over), start layering your coubliac: place 2 strips of salmon, 3 slices of hard boiled eggs, 3 thin slices of onion, and a good spread of sour cream. Repeat once. In a small bowl, whisk 2 eggs lightly. Egg wash the pastry all around the exposed edges with a pastry brush. Fold length side up first and tuck in ends. Egg wash all over. Bake at 400° for 25 minutes.

51

eve's downfall

Happy Apple Juice
Beef Benedict

Apple Juice
Cider
Apple Jack
Instant Sweetened
Ice Tea
Ground Sirloin
Eggs
White Bread
Hollandaise Sauce*
Mint Leaves

Happy Apple Juice

Mix 8 ounces apple juice, 8 ounces cider, 4 ounces apple jack and pour over ice in a pitcher. Add 2 teaspoons instant ice tea mix and several lemon slices. Refrigerate and serve in large ice tea glasses.

Beef Benedict

Toast 2 slices buttered bread. Broil 2 six-ounce ground sirloin beef patties, and set on toast. Fry 2 eggs and set one each on top of patty. Cover with Hollandaise sauce and minced mint.

*See recipe in Southern Gentleman

53

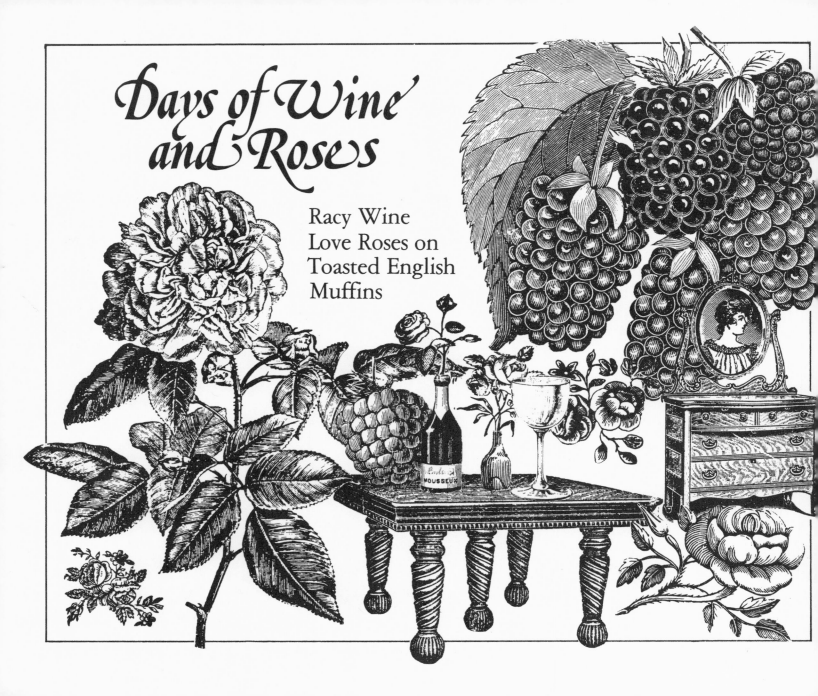

Days of Wine and Roses

Racy Wine
Love Roses on
Toasted English
Muffins

Red Wine
Raspberries
(fresh or frozen)
Medium Eggs
Chopped Parsley
Large Tomatoes
Cream
Flour
Tarragon
Hard Cheddar Cheese
English Muffins
Butter

Racy Wine

Place in blender 1 bottle of red wine (26 ounces) and 1 cup raspberries. Mix and chill. Serve in red wine glasses.

Love Roses on Toasted English Muffins

Blanch and peel 2 large tomatoes. Slice off tops and scoop out about 2 tablespoons of insides. In each hole, add 1/2 teaspoons butter and some chopped parsley, then add 1 raw egg. Replace tomato lid. Wrap in foil and set in small ramekins. Bake at 350° for 30 minutes.

Melt 2 tablespoons butter, add 2 tablespoons flour, and mix well. Add 1 cup cream, mixing slowly, then add tomato pulp plus 1 ounce hard cheddar cheese. Blend and heat.

Split one English muffin and toast. Remove tomatoes from foil and set on each muffin. Divide sauce over all and garnish with parsley.

55

fiery passion

Red Sea
Toast, Pimiento, Cheese, Caviar

Tomato Juice
Worcestershire Sauce
Tabasco
Lime Juice
Horseradish
Tequila
Shrimp
Bread
Pimiento
Fontina Cheese
Caviar

Red Sea

Chill 2 beautiful long-stem glasses. Add to each the following: 1 teaspoon Worcestershire sauce, 1/2 teaspoon Tabasco, 1 teaspoon white horseradish, 1 teaspoon lime juice, and fill to 3/4 full with tomato juice and 2 ounces tequila. Stir well and chill. At the last minute add ice cubes and garnish with a large cooked and peeled shrimp.

Toast, Pimiento, Cheese, Caviar

Toast 4 slices of white bread, trim crust, cover each with thin slices of fontina cheese, and cover lightly with caviar (lumpfish is OK). Place 4 thin strips of pimiento on each piece of toast. Lay out on baking sheet, and lay a piece of foil on top (do not tuck under). Bake at 350° for 25 minutes. Cut crosswise, and make a diamond shape with 4 pieces on each of the 2 plates.

57

Big Sur

Bellini
California
Omelette
Parsley Buttered Toast

Champagne
Brandy
Peaches (Fresh or
canned)
Eggs
Milk
Salt
Butter
Sour Cream
Strawberries
Banana
Melon
Grapes
Honey
Orange Juice
Lemon Rind
White Bread
Parsley

California Omelette

Separate 6 eggs. To the yolks add 1 teaspoon salt and beat. Beat egg whites until stiff and fold into egg yolks. Using an omelette pan, place 1 teaspoon butter and 1/2 of the egg mixture, cook for 2 minutes, add filling and flip 1/2 over to cover the filling. Repeat to make 2 omelettes.

Filling: Cut up 1 cup strawberries, 1 whole banana, 1/2 melon in cubes, and add seedless grapes. Set in bowl and marinate with 1 tablespoon honey and 1/2 cup orange juice. Top the omelets with sour cream and grated lemon rind.

Bellini

Place a whole peeled peach in each of 2 Pilsner glasses. Pour 2 teaspoons of brandy over each peach and let stand for a few minutes. Pour chilled Champagne into the glasses and serve with a tall spoon .

Parsley Buttered Toast

Melt 1/4 cup of butter, add 1 tablespoon finely chopped parsley and mix well. Toast 4 slices of white bread. Brush butter mixture onto the toast. Cut into triangles and wrap in a napkin to keep them warm.

59

Rendezvous

Lite Beer
Morning Paté with Corn Bread

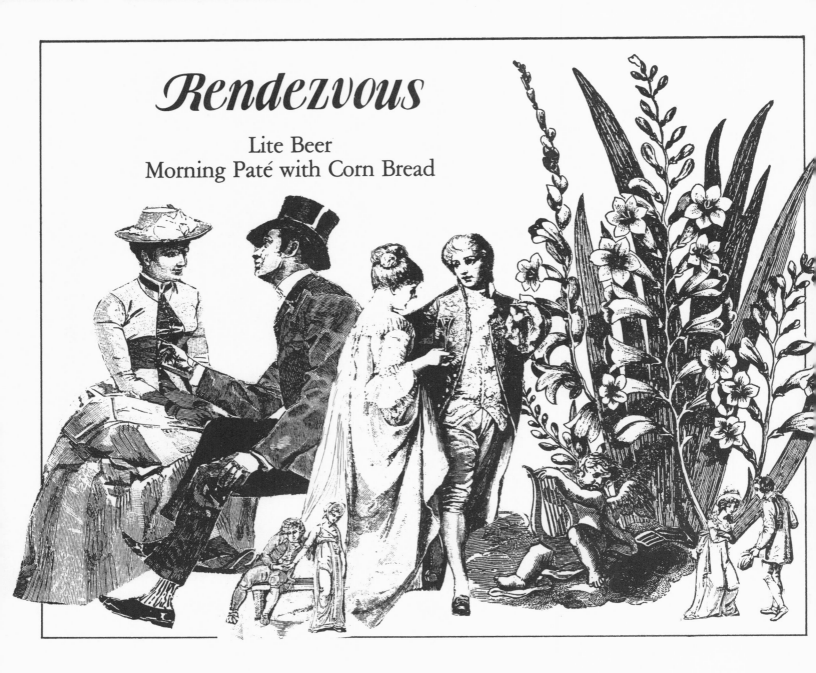

Lite Beer
Gelatin
Consomme
Catsup
Sherry
Vermouth
Horseradish
Salt
Mayonnaise
Hard Cooked Eggs
Pecans
Green Olives
Deviled Ham (or Tuna)
Corn Niblets
Onion
Bread Crumbs
Eggs
Milk
Marjoram
Pepper
Croutons

Morning Paté

In a saucepan, sprinkle 1 envelope of plain gelatin over 1/2 cup consomme. Let stand until soft. Put over low heat and stir constantly until gelatin dissolves. Remove from heat, add 1/2 cup more consomme, 1 tablespoon catsup, 2 tablespoons sherry, 2 tablespoons vermouth, 1/2 teaspoon horseradish, 1/2 cup mayonnaise, 1/4 cup sour cream, 6 hard cooked eggs in chunks, 1/2 cup green pitted olives, 1/4 cup pecans, 2 cans deviled ham or 1 can tuna. Mix well. Oil a mold, fill, packing well — cover — and *set overnight.* Unmold, and sprinkle with chopped parsley.

Corn Bread

Lightly brown in 1 tablespoon butter, 1 tablespoon minced onions, 2 cups corn niblets, 1 cup soft bread crumbs, 2 beaten eggs, 1 cup milk, 1 teaspoon salt, 1/2 teaspoon marjoram. Set into casserole and place in a pan of water (1/2 way up side of dish) sprinkle croutons over top. Bake at 350° for about 45 minutes.

Serve Lite beer in chilled pilsner glasses.

61

SUNRISE IN VERMONT

Sunshine Wine
Emperor's Pancakes

Apples
Honey
Walnuts
Oil
Cream
Maple Syrup
Flour
Eggs
White Wine
Cranberry Juice
Orange Juice

Emperor's Pancakes

In a blender, add 2 eggs, plus 2 egg yolks, 1/4 cup oil, 1/4 teaspoon salt, 1/2 cup flour, and 1/2 cup of cream. Blend well and chill for 30 minutes. Heat crepe skillet, oiling lightly. Add 2 tablespoons batter, and whirl around skillet for 2 minutes. Turn over and cook 1 minute. Repeat until you have 12 crepes. Set aside.

In a blender, add 4 peeled, cored, sliced apples, 1/2 cup maple syrup and 1/2 cup honey. Blend well. Add 1 cup of walnuts and blend 1/2 minute leaving nuts in small pieces.

Spread out crepes, frost with the apple mixture, and roll like cigars. Twist in crescent shape and have 6 form a circle like a crown on each plate. Set glass of Sunshine Wine in the middle of each crown and serve.

Sunshine Wine

In a blender, add 1 cup orange juice, 1 cup cranberry juice, 1 bottle white wine and 5 to 6 ice cubes. Blend until slushy. Pour into large red wine glasses.

63

Lovely Liason

Chablis
Cheese Soufflé
Melba Toast
Snappy Apples

Chablis
Milk
Butter
Cornstarch
Flour
Swiss Cheese
Eggs
Cayenne Pepper
Thinly Sliced Bread
Seasoned Salt
Apples
Chestnut Puree
Peach Jam
Heavy Cream
Lemon

Cheese Soufflé

Take a 1 quart soufflé dish and butter and dust with flour. Bring 12 ounces of milk to a boil and keep hot. In a sauce pan, melt 3 ounces of butter and add 2 tablespoons flour and 3 tablespoons cornstarch—mix together. Slowly add the hot milk, whisking constantly, until thick and smooth. Remove from heat and let cool. Add 4 egg yolks, one at a time, whisking in between. Add 4 ounces of diced Swiss cheese, and 1/2 teaspoon salt. Beat 4 egg whites and fold into sauce. Fill the souffle dish with the egg mixture. Place a 2 inch foil collar around the edge of the dish and tie with a string. Bake at 350° for 40 minutes.

Snappy Apples

Take 2 red apples, peel one-half way down and scoop out the core and seeds. Fill the cavity with chestnut puree and cover top with peach jam. Set in a pan, add a little water and bake at 250° for 1 hour. Top with whipped cream.

Melba Toast

Trim crust from 8 slices of thin bread and cut diagonally. Spread with melted butter and seasoned salt. Bake at 350° for 10 minutes.

Served chilled Chablis with lemon wedges in white wine glasses.

65

Canadian Courtship

Poached Pears in Wine
Breakfast Kedgeree
French Bread Slices

Red Wine
Pears
Cloves
Sour Cream
Cinnamon
Sugar
Rice
Smoked Haddock
Ham
Watercress
Butter
Cream
Eggs
French Bread
Tarragon
Salt

Poached Pears in Wine

In a sauce pan, put 1 small bottle of good red wine, heat and add 4 cloves and 2 large peeled pears (not cored). Gently simmer until tender. Place pears into 2 soup bowls and top with the wine and a big scoop of sour cream. Sprinkle cinnamon and sugar on top.

Breakfast Kedgeree

In a large bowl, mix 1-1/2 cups of cooked rice, 1/2 cup smoked haddock (cut into small pieces), 1/2 pound cooked ham (cut into small pieces), 1/4 cup chopped watercress, 1/4 cup melted butter, and 1/4 cup cream. Place in a casserole dish, top with sliced hard boiled eggs. Cover tightly with foil and bake at 350° for 20 minutes.

French Bread Slices

Slice a small loaf of French bread into many slices. Melt 1/4 cup of butter, add 1/2 teaspoons salt, 1/2 teaspoons tarragon. Dip each slice into butter mixture and lay out onto sheets. Bake in 350° oven for 15 to 20 minutes.

67

Georgia on My Mind

Bourbon Punch

Potato Cakes, Eggs
and Peanut Sauce

Bourbon
French Coffee
(or strong American)
Heavy Cream
Sugar
Potatoes
Onions
Eggs
Baking Powder
Salt Peanuts
Garlic
Soy Sauce
Brown Sugar
Tabasco Sauce
Cinnamon
French Fried Onion
Rings (canned)
Milk

Bourbon Punch
Place 1 cup bourbon, 1 cup coffee, and 1 cup cream in a blender. Add 1 tablespoon sugar, and blend. Pour into pan and heat. Serve hot with whipped cream and cinnamon.

Potato Cakes and Eggs
Place in a food processor 3 peeled and cubed raw potatoes, 2 eggs, 1/2 cup flour, 1 small onion, 1 teaspoon salt, 1/4 teaspoon baking powder — mix well. Lightly oil a skillet, and when hot, spoon batter out like pancakes. Turn and brown on both sides. Makes about 4.

Fry 4 eggs sunny side up, and set one on each potato cake. Pour sauce over.

Peanut Sauce
In a food processor, add 1 can French fried onion rings, 1 cup peanuts, 1 cup water, 2 tablespoons soy sauce, 2 tablespoons brown sugar, a dash of tabasco, and blend well. Add 2 tablespoons milk, and blend again. Place into pot, heat and serve in a pitcher to pour over potato cakes and eggs.

69

Pas de Deux

Wild Strawberry Wine
Eggs Poached in Maple Syrup
on Real French Toast

Strawberry Liqueur
White Wine
Eggs
Maple Syrup
French Bread
Cream
Butter

Real French Toast
Slice two - 6'' pieces of French bread lengthwise. Beat 2 eggs with 1 tablespoon cream. Dip bread in egg and fry with melted butter. When golden brown, set in oven to keep hot.

Eggs Poached in Maple Syrup
In a skillet, heat 2 cups maple syrup and slip 4 eggs in very gently. Cook 6 minutes. Remove toast from oven, set on plates and, with slotted spoon, remove eggs putting 1 on each piece of toast. Use warm maple syrup over all.

Wild Strawberry Wine
In a pitcher, pour 1 bottle white wine and 1 cup strawberry liqueur. Stir. Fill 2 wine glasses with crushed ice and pour over.

71